This book belongs to

Chloe

RUN, BUG, RUN!

a collection of short stories

Second Edition

Copyright © 2016 by All About® Learning Press, Inc.
Previous editions copyright © 2010-2015
Printed in the United States of America

Second Edition
v. 2.0.0

All About® Learning Press, Inc.
615 Commerce Loop
Eagle River, WI 54521
www.AllAboutReading.com
ISBN 978-1-935197-65-2

Stories:

Marie Rippel:	"Bam" – "The Cat" – "Jam" – "A Hat" – "Hit the Gas" "The Bad Rat" – "The Job" – "Jan Did It" – "Run, Bug, Run!" "Kip the Pup" – "The Gum" – "Pet Ox" – "Fox in a Box" "The Red Pen" – "Run!" – "The Tub"
Renée LaTulippe:	"The Sad Hog" – "Get Them!" – "Six Fish" "Get the Moth, Meg!"

Illustrations:

Matt Chapman:	"The Bad Rat" – "The Gum" – "Fox in a Box" "The Red Pen"
Donna Goeddaeus:	"Bam" – "The Cat" – "A Hat" – "Hit the Gas" – "The Job" "Jan Did It" – "Run, Bug, Run!" – "Kip the Pup" – "The Sad Hog" "Pet Ox" – "Get Them!" – "Run!" – "Six Fish" – "The Tub"
Dave LaTulippe:	"Jam" – "Get the Moth, Meg!"

Contributors:	Donna Goeddaeus, Samantha Johnson
Cover Design:	Dave LaTulippe
Page Layout:	Andy Panske

Run, Bug, Run!: a collection of short stories is part of the *All About® Reading* program.

For more books in this series, go to www.AllAboutReading.com.

To the reader –
may you discover the joy in reading!

Contents

Bam!

Pat.

Tap. Tap. Tap.

Tap the map.

Tap. Tap. Tap.

Tap the jam.

Tap the pan.

Bam!

The End

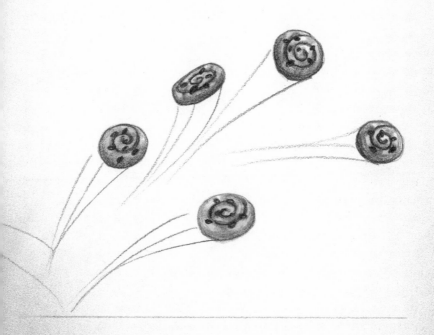

The Cat

Sam sat.

The cat sat.

The cat can bat at the tag.

Mad Sam!

Bad cat!

Nap!

The End

Jam

Pam sat.

The yak sat.

Pam had ham.

The yak had ham.

Pam had a yam.

The yak had a yam.

Pam had jam.

The yak had jam.

The yak had JAM!

Pam had a bag.

The bag had jam!

Jam! Jam! Jam!

The End

The man had a hat.

The ram had a hat.

The yak had a hat.

The bat had a hat.

The cat had a hat.

The rat had a hat.

The hat had a hat!

The End

Hit the Gas

Vic had a map.

Vic sat in the van.

Kip sat in the van.

The ram fit in the van.

The pig sat in the van.

Did the van tip a bit?

Zip!

The rat hid in the van.

Hit the gas, Vic!

The End

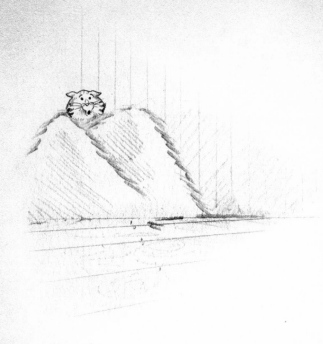

The Bad Rat

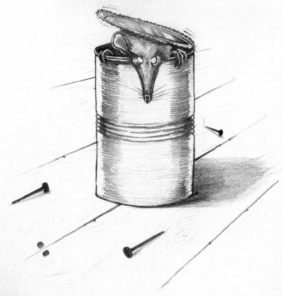

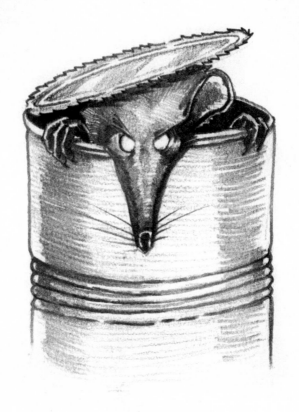

The bad rat hid

in the tin can.

The rat bit the pig.

The pig bit the cat.

The cat bit Jim.

Jim hit the fan.

The fan hit the rat.

Bam!

The rat hid
in the tin can.

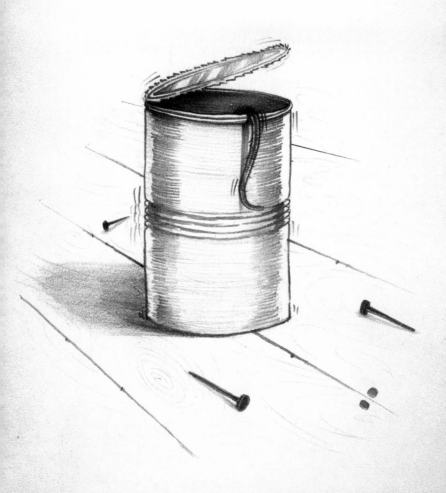

The End

Jan Did It

Did Jan jog?

Jan did!

Did Jan hop?

Jan did!

Did Jan mop?

Jan did!

Did Jan dig?

Jan did!

Did Jan jig?

Jan did!

Did Jan sob?

Jan did *not*!

The End

The Job

Lad got a hot dog.

Lad got pop.

Lad had a job.

"Lad, hop in."

"Sip the pop, Lad!"

"Sit, Lad!"

Lad sat.

Lad got the hot dog.

Lad got in an ad!

The End

Run, Bug, Run!

The bug sat on a bud.

Run, bug, run!

The bug sat on a mug.

Run, bug, run!

The bug got up on a log.

Run, bug, run!

The bug sat on a big dog.

Run, bug, run!

The bug sat on a rug.

Run, bug, run!

The bug hid in a jug.

Run, bug, run!

The bug is in a big mob.

The bug did not run!

The End

Kip the Pup

Kip is a pup.

Yup, yup, yup!

Kip sat in the sun.

The pup got hot.

Tug, tug, tug!

Kip had fun!

Kip sat in the hut.

Sit, sit, sit!

The pup sat up.

Kip got in the pot.

Dig, dig, dig!

The pup dug in the mud.

Kip sat in his tub.

Rub, rub, rub!

Kip got a rub in his tub.

Bud got the pup.

Hug, hug, hug!

Yip, yip, yip!

The End

The Gum

Peg got gum on the rug.

Ted got a wet rag.

Ted did not get the gum.

Ed got a mop.

Ed did not get the gum.

Dad dug at the gum.

Dad did not get the gum.

Mom got a log. Mom hit the gum.

Mom did not get the gum.

Jen got a pig.

The pig got the gum.

Yum!

The End

The Sad Hog

Val had a sad hog.

The hog sat in the mud pit.

Val sat in the mud pit.

The hog let Val hug him.

Val got a wig.

Val set the wig on top of the hog.

The wig fit!

Val got a hat.

Val set the hat on the wig.

The hat fit!

Val got a fan.

Val got a red bud.

The hog had fun.

Val had fun.

Val got a hug.

The hog is *not* sad!

The End

Pet Ox

Jax has a pet ox.

The ox is not as big as Jax.

The ox got in the den.

The ox got on the bed.

The ox got wet.

Mom is not mad—yet!

"Jax! Get the ox in his pen!"

Run, ox!

Run, Jax!

The End

Fox in a Box

Fox has a box.

Fox is in the box.

Fox is on the box.

The box is on Fox.

The box is *in* Fox!

Quit it, Fox!

Can Fox fix the box?

Fox did not fix the box!

The End

Get Them!

A bun!

Can the pug get it?

The pug can hop up.

Up.

Up!

Up!

The pug did not get the bun.

The pug can get on this man.

thud!

The pug did the math.

The pug can get ...

this man,

that man,

a thin man,

a big man!

Then the pug can nab that bun!

"The pug has the bun!"

The men ran.

The pug ran with the bun.

"Get them!"

The End

The Red Pen

This is Tex.

Tex is a thin red pen.

Tex is a big, big hen.

Tex is a net with a bug in it.

Tex is a jet with an X on it.

Tex is a fox in the bath.

Tex is a box on the path.

Tex is a log in a bog.

Tex is a big red dog.

Tex is a fun kid!

178

Run!

Is that a cub?

Run! Dash up the path!

Run, run, run!

Run on the log!

Get in the shed!

Shut the shed! Lash it shut!

Hush!

Is that a cub?

It is Mom!

The End

Six Fish

Beth did a job with Josh.

Beth did a job with Ash.

Beth did a job with Dad.

Beth got cash.

Beth can shop!

Did Beth get a cat?

Did Beth get a dog?

Did Beth get a fish?

Yes! Beth got six fish!

The End

The Tub

Chad had a pal, Rich.

Rich had a big tub.

This tub is fun!

Chad set a big ship in the tub.

The ship did a lap.

Rich set his pig on the ship.

Chug! Chug! Chug!

Chad set fish in the tub.

The fish did a zig-zag.

Rich got in the tub!

This tub *is* fun!

The End

Get the Moth, Meg!

Sh!

A moth is on the dish.

Can Meg get it with a net?

Meg got Dad with the net!

Meg did not get the moth.

That bad moth!

It is in the bath.

It is on the tap.

Meg has a wish—

get this moth with the net!

The moth is on a nut.

Meg can get it!

Zig! Zag!

Meg did not get the moth.

This is not much fun!

Meg is mad!

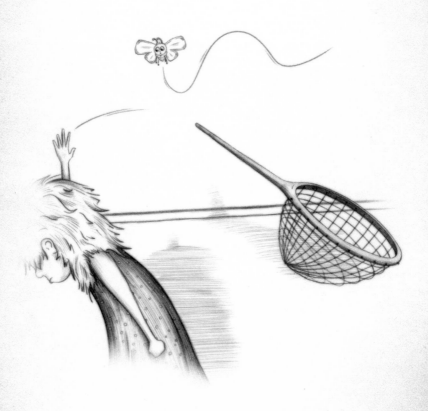

Meg has had it!

Meg did not get the moth.

But the moth got the net!

The End

Good job!

You've read about boxes and foxes

and a hog in a wig ...

Now you're ready

to read *The Runt Pig*!